1925) called his spiritual philosophy 'anthroposophy', meaning 'wisdom of the human being'. As a highly developed seer, he based his work on direct knowledge and perception of spiritual dimensions. He initiated a modern and universal 'science of spirit', accessible to anyone willing to exercise clear and unprejudiced thinking.

From his spiritual investigations Steiner provided suggestions for the renewal of many activities, including education (both general and special), agriculture, medicine, economics, architecture, science, philosophy, religion and the arts. Today there are thousands of schools, clinics, farms and other organizations involved in practical work based on his principles. His many published works feature his research into the spiritual nature of the human being, the evolution of the world and humanity, and methods of personal development. Steiner wrote some 30 books and delivered over 6000 lectures across Europe. In 1924 he founded the General Anthroposophical Society, which today has branches throughout the world.

EDUCATING CHILDREN TODAY

RUDOLF STEINER

Sophia Books

Sophia Books
An imprint of Rudolf Steiner Press
Hillside House, The Square
Forest Row RH18 5ES

www.rudolfsteinerpress.com

Published by Rudolf Steiner Press 2008

First published in a translation by George and Mary Adams by
Rudolf Steiner Press in 1981

This translation revised by Matthew Barton
© Rudolf Steiner Press 2008

Originally published in German as part of the volume entitled
Lucifer-Gnosis (volume 34 in the *Rudolf Steiner Gesamtausgabe*
or Collected Works) by Rudolf Steiner Verlag, Dornach. This
authorized translation is published by permission of the Rudolf
Steiner Nachlassverwaltung, Dornach

A catalogue record for this book is available from the British
Library

ISBN 978 185584 206 9

Cover by Andrew Morgan
Typeset by DP Photosetting, Neath, West Glamorgan
Printed and bound in Great Britain by Cromwell Press Limited,
Trowbridge, Wiltshire

Contents

Note to the German edition, 1909

The following text is based on the substance of a lecture which I gave at various places in Germany. I have here refashioned it in essay form in response to requests for a printed version. The reader's attention is drawn to footnotes which have now been added.

Rudolf Steiner

Contemporary life is calling into question much that we have inherited from past generations—giving rise to the many 'contemporary issues' and 'needs of the time' we keep hearing about. There are so many of these 'issues': the Social Question, the Women's Question, various questions about education and schooling, questions of human rights and health issues, to name but a few. People are attempting to grapple with these problems in all kinds of ways. The number of those who offer this or that remedy or solution—or partial solution—is beyond counting. In the process all shades of opinion come to the fore: radicalism, with its revolutionary stance; moderate liberalism which maintains respect for what already exists, but tries to develop something new from

1

it; and conservatism, which is up in arms whenever any of the old institutions and traditions seem under threat. All sorts of other, intermediate positions exist alongside these main tendencies.

Looking at all these phenomena with deeper insight we cannot help feeling that our time often fails to meet contemporary needs with adequate means. Many wish to introduce reforms without really knowing life's deeper foundations. Whoever wishes to propose solutions for the future, however, cannot be satisfied with a superficial knowledge of life, but must explore its deeper aspects.

The whole of life is like a plant, containing not just what it presents outwardly but also a future state concealed in its depths. If you look at a plant just coming into leaf you can be sure that after a while the leaf-bearing stem will also put forth flowers and fruit. In its hidden depths the plant already contains the disposition to produce flowers and fruit; but if you restrict your judgement to what the plant now presents to outward sight, how would you ever know what its new organs will look like? Only someone who familiarizes himself with the *essence* of the plant, its deeper nature, can know such a thing.

Likewise, the whole of human life contains the germs of its own future within it. But if we are to know anything about this future state, we must first explore the hidden nature of the human being—which our age is little inclined to do. Instead it concerns itself with what appears on the surface, and thinks that trying to engage with what is hidden from external observation is treading on shaky ground.

Things are of course a good deal simpler in the case of a plant. We know that others like it have in the past repeatedly borne fruit. A human life, on the other hand, is present only once, and the blossom it will bear in future has never previously appeared. Yet it is germinally present in us just as flowers exist in a plant that is still only in leaf.

It is in fact possible to say something about our future if we dig down beneath the surface of human nature and penetrate to its essence. Only deeper insight into human life will enable the various ideas for social reform to become really fruitful and practical.

It is intrinsic to the science of the spirit that it must offer a practical view of the world—one that takes full account of the nature and essence of human life. Whether what people often call spiritual science is worthy of the name in this respect is not the point. We are here concerned with the essence of spiritual science, and its true potential. Anthroposophy[1] is not intended to be an abstract, lifeless theory that caters only for people's curiosity; nor is it meant to be a means by which just a few people try, selfishly, to attain a higher level of self-development for themselves alone. What it *can* do is collaborate on solving the most important tasks of contemporary humanity, and supporting developments which enhance human well-being.[2]

In taking on this task, it is true, anthroposophy must be prepared to face all kinds of scepticism and opposition. Radicals, moderates and conservatives in every sphere of life will inevitably regard it with scepticism. To start with it will scarcely be in a position to meet with favour from any partisan tendency, since its concerns lie far beyond the thrust of party politics and are rooted solely in a true knowledge and perception of life.

Those who have insight into life will create the tasks they set themselves in accordance with life itself. They will not plan arbitrary reform programmes, since they will know that the fundamental laws of life prevailing today will still apply in the future. Spiritual researchers will therefore inevitably respect what already exists. However great the need for improvement they find in the present, they will see latent in it the germ of the future. But they will also know that all development requires growth and evolution, and thus find in what already exists the seeds of

5

this transformation and growth. They will not *invent* programmes of reform but will read them out of what is already there. What is read in this way will in a sense itself become a programme of reform, bearing within itself the very nature of development. This is why anthroposophical insight into the essential nature of the human being will offer the most practical means for solving urgent contemporary problems.

In what follows I will try to show this in a particular instance—in relation to education. Rather than making demands and establishing programmes I will simply describe the nature of the child. What is inherent in the growing and evolving human being will itself provide the perspective from which to develop education.

If we wish to perceive the characteristics of the developing human being, we must start by considering the hidden nature of the human being *per se*. What sensory observation discovers in the human being and what a materialistic view of life considers to be the one and only aspect is to spiritual investigation solely one part, one aspect of his nature. This is the physical body. Our physical body is subject to the same laws of physical existence and is built up from the same substances and forces as the whole of the rest of the so-called lifeless or mineral realm. Spiritual science therefore tells us that we have a physical body in common with the whole mineral kingdom; and in this view the term 'physical body' only denotes what combines these same substances, according to the same laws as are at work in the mineral kingdom, to create the human form and dissolve this again.

Over and above this physical body, anthroposophy also recognizes a second essential principle in the human being. This is our etheric or life body. Physicists should not take offence at the term 'etheric body'—the word 'ether' here does not mean the same in this context as the hypothetical ether of physics. The phrase should be taken only to mean what will now be described.

In recent times it was considered highly unscientific to speak of an 'etheric body', although this was not the case at the end of the eighteenth and during the first half of the nineteenth century. In those days people recognized that the substances and forces at work in a mineral cannot by themselves form the mineral into a living creature. In the latter, therefore, they thought that a special 'force' must reside, which they called 'the vital force', thinking of it somewhat as follows. The vital force is active in plants, animals and humans, and produces the phenomena of life, just as the magnetic force is present in a magnet and produces the phenomenon of attraction. But as materialism developed, people relinquished this idea. People began to say that living creatures develop in the same way as so-called lifeless minerals, and contain no other forces than those at work in them. In this view of things, these forces simply interact in a more complex way and create a more intricate structure.

Nowadays, however, only the most insistent materialists still adhere to this denial of a life force or vital force. There are a number of scientists and thinkers who have discovered in the facts themselves that something like a vital force or life principle must be assumed. Thus, in its most recent developments, and drawing on its sensory observations and logical reflections, modern science is starting to assume the existence of a kind of life force. However, this is not the method of genuine spiritual investigation which spiritual science adopts, and the results of which inform what it says. It cannot be stressed enough how great the difference is, in this respect, between spiritual science and modern natural science. The latter regards sensory experience as the foundation of all knowledge. Anything not based on this foundation it assumes to be unknowable, for all its deductions and conclusions are drawn from sensory impressions. All that is not composed of such impressions is relegated to a sphere 'beyond the frontiers of human knowledge'.

From the perspective of spiritual science this view is like that of a blind person who only admits the validity of things he can touch, and conclusions based on this sense of touch: someone, in other words, who rejects what sighted people state about the world as lying beyond the bounds of human knowledge. Spiritual science shows us to be capable of evolution, of bringing new worlds into view by developing new organs of perception. A blind person is surrounded by light and colour, but he cannot see them because he lacks the necessary organs. In the same way anthroposophy holds that the human being is surrounded by many worlds, which we can perceive if we develop the organs needed to do so. Just as a blind person who undergoes a successful operation looks out on a new world, so by developing higher organs we can come to know new worlds altogether different from those we can perceive through our ordinary senses.

Whether someone who is blind can be operated on depends on his organs of sight. But the higher organs which allow us to penetrate into higher worlds are germinally present in every person. Everyone can develop them with the patience, persistence and energy needed to apply in his own case the methods described in the volume *Knowledge of the Higher Worlds*.[3]

Spiritual science never says, therefore, that there are definite boundaries to human knowledge. It prefers to say that the human being can be aware of the existence of worlds for which he has the organs of perception; and it speaks only of the methods whereby existing frontiers can be extended. This is its position, too, when it comes to investigating the life body or etheric body, and all that the following pages contain in relation to still higher aspects of the human being. It accepts that the physical body alone is accessible to enquiry through the physical senses and that—as far as this kind of enquiry is concerned—the most we can do is surmise the existence of higher bodies by intellectual deductions. At the same time, though, it explains how a world can open up in which the observer perceives the higher aspects of human nature, just as colour and light appear to a person born blind who successfully undergoes an operation to restore his sight. For those who have developed higher organs of perception, the etheric or life body is an object of perception and not just of intellectual deduction.

We have the etheric or life body in common with plants and animals. The life body works in a formative way on the physical body's substances and forces, thus bringing about the phenomena of growth, reproduction and inner circulation of fluids, etc. It therefore builds the physical body, both forming and dwelling in it. We can even say that the physical body is an image or expression of the life body. In human beings the form and size of both are approximately, though certainly not exactly, equal. In animals however, and still more so in plants, the etheric body is very different, both in form and extent, from the physical.

The third aspect of the human being is what we call the sentient or astral body. This is the vehicle of pain and pleasure, of impulse, craving, passion and the like—all of which are absent in a creature consisting only of physical and etheric bodies.[4] These passions and drives are all encompassed in the word *sentience*. The plant has no such feeling. If some academics conclude that plants have a certain capacity to feel from the fact that they respond by movement or in some other way to an external stimulus, they only show their ignorance of the nature of sentience. The point is not whether something responds to an external stimulus, but whether the stimulus is reflected in an *inner* process—as pain, pleasure, impulse, desire or the like. Unless we hold fast to this, we would be justified in saying that blue litmus paper feels certain sub-

13

stances because it turns red on contact with them.[5]

We therefore have a sentient body in common with the animal kingdom only, and this sentient body is the vehicle of sensation or sentient life.

We should not, as certain theosophical circles do, erroneously conceive the etheric and sentient bodies as consisting simply of finer, more rarefied substances than are present in the physical body, for that is a materialistic view of these higher aspects of our nature. The etheric body is, rather, a form composed of forces. It consists of active forces, not matter. And the astral or sentient body is a figure of inwardly moving, coloured and luminous images.[6]

The astral body deviates both in size and shape from the physical body. In the human beings it appears as an elongated ovoid form, in which both the physical and etheric bodies are embedded, and projects beyond them as a vivid, luminous form on all sides.

Now we also possess a fourth dimension to our

being, which no other earthly creature has. This is the vehicle or bearer of the human 'I' or ego. The little word 'I'—as used in English for example—is a name essentially different from all other names. Anyone who rightly ponders the nature of this name can gain direct insight into the essence of human nature. All other names can be used by all people equally to denote what they refer to, but this is not true of the word 'I'. No one can use this name to refer to another person, but can only use it to speak of himself. The name 'I' can never reach my ears from without to denote myself. In calling himself 'I', a person names himself within himself, so that a being who can say 'I' is a world in himself. Religions founded on knowledge of the spirit have always had a strong sense of this, saying that the 'God' who in lower creatures reveals himself only from without, in external phenomena, begins to speak from within in the 'I'. The bearer of this capacity to say 'I', the ego faculty, is the 'I body', the fourth aspect of our being.[7]

This 'I body' or 'I-bearer' is the vehicle of our higher soul, and makes us the crown of all earthly creation. Now in modern people the I or ego is by no means simple in nature. We can recognize its character if we compare human beings at different stages of development. For instance one might compare a member of a tribal community living in the wilds of nature, an average European, and a lofty idealist. Each of them has the capacity to say 'I' to himself and the I-bearer is present in all. But the tribesman uses his I to pursue an almost animal-like capacity of instinct, passions and environmental response.[8] The more cultured European has such desires and passions too, but while he allows himself to follow some, there are others which he reins in and suppresses. The idealist has developed new, higher desires and passions in addition to the ones originally present, which have arisen through the I working on the other bodies. In fact, this is the ego's precise and particular task: autonomously to refine and

16

purify the other aspects or bodies which constitute us.

Thus the lower bodies of someone who has developed beyond the state with which he is first endowed by nature are to a greater or lesser degree transformed under the ego's influence. When we are just beginning to rise above an animal-like state, when our ego is only just kindling, our lower bodies still resemble those of an animal. Our etheric or life body is then simply the vehicle of life's formative forces, of growth and reproduction. Our sentient body gives expression only to the impulses, desires and passions which our environment elicits from us. As we work our way beyond this stage through successive lives or incarnations to ever higher evolution, the ego works upon and transforms our other bodies. In this way the sentient body becomes the vehicle of purified sensations of pleasure and pain, refined wishes and desires. And the etheric or life body is also transformed, to become the bearer of our habits, our more

17

permanent tendencies in life, of our temperament and memory. A person whose ego has not yet worked upon his life body has no memories of the experiences he undergoes in life, but just lives out what nature has implanted in him.

This is what the growth and development of civilization means for the human being: a continual working of our ego upon the lower aspects of our nature. This work penetrates right down into the physical body. Under the influence of the ego the whole appearance and physiognomy, the gestures and movements of the physical body, are altered. It is also possible to distinguish how different modes of culture and education work on each body or sheath of our being. Ordinary cultural influences work on the sentient body and imbue it with pleasures, pains, impulses and desires which are different in kind from those originally innate to it. When a person is absorbed in contemplation of a great work of art, this influences and affects his etheric body. Through the work of art he divines something higher and more noble than his ordinary sensory environment offers, and in this process he forms and transforms his life body. Religion is a powerful means for purifying and ennobling the etheric body, and thus it offers a great impetus for the evolution of humanity.

What we call 'conscience' is nothing other than the outcome of the ego's work on the life body through a series of incarnations. When people realize that they ought not to do this or that, and when this insight makes such a strong impact on them that its impression enters their etheric body, then 'conscience' arises.

Now this work of the ego or 'I' on the lower aspects of our human constitution can either be an achievement possessed in common by the whole human race or else can be entirely individual, an achievement of an individual ego working on itself alone. In the former case the whole of humanity collaborates, as it were, on transforming the human being. The latter kind of transformation depends on the activity of the individual ego alone and by itself. The ego may become so strong as to transform the sentient body by its own power and strength. This ego-transformed sentient or astral body is called Spirit Self (or the eastern term 'manas') and is mainly wrought through a process of learning, of enriching one's inner life with higher ideas and perceptions.

Now the ego can rise to still higher, primary and intrinsic work on the essential human self. This occurs when, besides ennobling the astral body, the etheric or life body is also transformed. We learn many things in the course of our lives; and if at some point we look back on our past life we may reflect that we have learned a great deal. Only to a much lesser extent, though, will we be able to say that we have transformed our temperament or character during life, or have improved our memory. Learning concerns the astral body whereas these later kinds of transformation concern the etheric or life body. Thus it is really quite appropriate if we compare the change in the astral body during life with the movement of a clock's minute hand and the transformation of the life body with the much slower movement of the hour hand.

When we embark on higher or so-called esoteric training, it is this latter transformation which we should undertake above all, through the intrinsic and autonomous power of the ego. Individually and in full consciousness we should work on transforming our habits, temperament, character and memory. To the extent that we work upon our life body in this way, we transform it into what in anthroposophical terminology is called Life Spirit (or the eastern term 'buddhi').

At a still higher stage we can acquire the forces to work upon our physical body and transform it (for example transforming blood circulation and pulse). The transformed physical body is called Spirit Man (or the eastern term 'atma').

Now as a member of the whole human race or

of some part of it—for example a nation, blood relations or family group—we also, as a whole community, achieve certain transformations of the lower bodies. In spiritual science the following names are given to this kind of transformation. The ego-transformed astral or sentient body is called the sentient soul, the transformed etheric body is called the mind or intellectual soul, and the transformed physical body is called the consciousness soul. We should not imagine that transformation of these three constituent aspects takes place one after another in chronological sequence. From the moment the ego or 'I' lights up, all three bodies start being transformed simultaneously. In fact, the work of the ego does not become clearly apparent until a part of the consciousness soul has already formed and developed.

Thus we can speak of four bodies that constitute us: the physical body, the etheric or life body, the astral or sentient body and the ego or I body.

The sentient soul, the mind soul and the consciousness soul, and beyond these still higher constituents of our being—Spirit Self, Life Spirit and Spirit Man—appear as transformation of the original four bodies. When we speak of the bearers of human characteristics, these four bodies are really all that we need to consider.

As educator one works on these four aspects of the human being. Hence if we wish to work in the right way we have to discover their attributes. We mustn't imagine that they develop uniformly in the human being so that at any given point in his life—the moment of birth for instance—they are all equally developed. No, their development occurs differently at different stages of life. We need to be aware of these laws of human development if we are to approach education and also the school curriculum in the right way.

Before physical birth the growing human being is surrounded on all sides by the physical body of another. He does not enter into direct,

23

autonomous contact with the physical world. His mother's body is his physical environment, and this body alone is what works upon him as he grows and matures. In fact, physical birth consists in the liberation of the human being from the enclosing body of the mother, thus enabling the physical environment to work upon him more directly. His senses open to the outer world, and the outer world thus acquires an influence on the human being which was previously exercised by the enclosing, physical sheath of his mother's body.

A spiritual understanding of the world, such as that embodied in spiritual science, regards this as the birth of the physical, but not yet of the etheric or life body. Just as we are surrounded until the moment of birth by the physical enclosure of our mother's body, so, until the time of the change of teeth—around the age of seven—we are surrounded and protected by an enclosing etheric and astral integument. It is only during the change of teeth that this etheric enclosure allows the etheric body to emerge. And an astral enclosure remains until puberty, when the astral or sentient body is emancipated on all sides, just as the physical body was emancipated at birth and the etheric body at the change of teeth.[9]

Thus spiritual science must speak of *three births* of the human being. Until the change of teeth, certain impressions intended for the etheric body can as little reach it as the light and air of the physical world can reach the physical body of the embryo enclosed in the mother's womb.

Before the change of teeth occurs, the free life body is not yet working upon the human being. In the same way as the physical embryo in the mother's body receives forces which are not its own, and at the same time gradually develops its own forces within the protective enclosure of the mother's womb, so the same is true of the forces of growth up to the change of teeth. During this time the etheric body is first unfolding its own forces in conjunction with those it has inherited, which are not its own. While the etheric body is working towards its emancipation, the physical body is already autonomous. As it emancipates itself, the etheric body unfolds and develops what it can give to the physical body. The second teeth—which are in fact the human being's own, intrinsic teeth—replace those which he inherited, and represent the culmination of this preceding work. Embedded most densely in the physical body, they are last to appear at the end and as the culmination of this period.

From this moment on, our own etheric body is solely responsible for growth. But this etheric body is still under the influence of an astral body that remains within its protective integument. At the moment the astral body is also set free, the etheric body concludes another developmental stage, which finds its expression in puberty. The organs of reproduction become autonomous because from this time on the emancipated astral body no longer works inwards, but directly and without protection enters into engagement with the outer world.

Now just as the physical influences of the outer world cannot yet be brought to bear directly on an unborn child, so until the change of teeth we should not bring to bear on the etheric body the forces which, for it, correspond to the impressions of the physical environment on the physical body. And likewise the corresponding influences should not be brought to bear on the astral body until after puberty.

Vague and general phrases such as 'harmonious development of the child's innate powers and talents' cannot provide the basis for a genuine art of education, which depends on real knowledge of the human being. It is not that such phrases are wrong, but that they are as useless as saying that all parts of a machine must be made to work together harmoniously. To make a machine work you have to apply real, detailed knowledge, not phrases and truisms.

For the art of education likewise, what is important is specific insight into the way the human being is constituted, and how each aspect develops. We need to know what part of the human constitution we should work on at a certain age, and how we can properly do so. There is no doubt, of course, that an art of education geared to human realities, such as suggested here, will only slowly come about. This is due to the whole outlook of our age which will long continue to regard spiritual realities as the vaporous chimeras of an imagination run wild, while regarding vague and altogether unreal phrases as proof of a realistic way of thinking. Here, though, I will unreservedly describe what will in time come to be a matter of common knowledge, though today many people still regard it as a figment of the imagination.

With physical birth the human body is exposed to the physical environment of the external world. Before birth it was surrounded by the protecting enclosure of the mother's body. What the forces and fluids of the enveloping mother body have previously done for it must from then on be accomplished for it by the forces and elements of the outer physical world. Then, up to the change of teeth in the seventh year, the human body must of itself perform a task which is essentially different from tasks involved at all other periods of life. During this period the physical organs must take on certain shapes. Their structural relationships must acquire certain tendencies and orientations. Growth also takes place at later periods, but throughout the rest of life it is based on the forms which developed during this initial period. If forms have developed properly, proper forms will continue to grow later. If misshapen forms develop, then misshapen forms will grow subsequently. We can never repair what we, as carers and educators, have neglected in the first seven years. Just as nature brings about the right environment for the physical human body before birth, so after birth the parent and educator must create the right physical environment. It is the right physical environment alone which works upon the child in such a way that the physical organs shape themselves in the right way.

Two magic words indicate how the young child enters into relationship with his environment. These are: imitation and example. The Greek philosopher Aristotle called the human being the most imitative of the animals. This is truer of the first stage of childhood, before the change of teeth, than of any other period of life. The child imitates what occurs in his physical environment, and in the process of imitation his physical organs are cast into the forms which then assume permanence. 'Physical environment' must however be taken in the widest conceivable sense. It includes not only what goes on around the child in a material sense but everything that takes place in the child's environment—everything which his senses can perceive, which can work from the physical space surrounding him upon his inner spiritual forces. This also includes all the moral or immoral actions, all the wise or foolish actions that the child sees.

Moral admonitions or reasoned instructions do not influence the child in this way, but rather what adults actually do visibly before a child's eyes. The effect of admonition is to mould the forms not of the physical but of the etheric body; and the latter, as we saw, is surrounded until the age of seven or so by an enclosing etheric protection, just as the physical body is enclosed protectively in the mother's body until the moment of birth. All that needs to evolve in the etheric body up to the age of seven—ideas, habits, memories and so forth—must develop 'of its own accord', just as the eyes and ears develop within the mother's body without the influence of external light. What Jean Paul writes in his excellent educational work entitled *Levana, or, Education* is undoubtedly true.[10] He

31

says that a traveller learns more from his nurse in the first years of his life than in all his journeys round the world. The child, however, does not learn by instruction or admonition but by imitation. The physical organs shape their forms through the influence of the physical environment. The child will develop good sight if his environment has the right conditions of light and colour, while the physical foundations for a healthy moral sense will be laid in the brain and blood circulation if the child sees moral actions in his environment. If, before the age of seven, the child only sees foolish actions in his surroundings, the brain will assume forms that predispose it to foolishness in later life.

As the muscles of the hand grow firm and strong by performing the work for which they are fitted, so the brain and other organs of the human physical body are guided into proper lines of development if they receive the right impressions from their environment. An example will best illustrate this. You can make a doll for a child by folding up an old napkin, making two corners into legs, the other corners into arms, a knot for the head, then painting eyes, nose and mouth with blobs of ink. Or you can instead buy the child what they call a 'pretty doll' with real hair and painted cheeks. We need not dwell on the fact that the 'pretty doll' is of course hideous and apt to spoil a person's healthy aesthetic sense for life. The main educational question is a different one. If the child has the folded napkin as doll, he has to fill out with his own imagination everything needed to make it real and human for him. This work of the imagination moulds and forms the brain. The brain develops in the same way that the muscles of the hand develop when they do the work for which they are fitted. But give the child the so-called 'pretty doll' and the brain has nothing more to do. Instead of developing, it becomes stunted and dried up. If people could see into the brain as the spiritual investigator can, and see how it builds its forms, they would assuredly give their children only the kinds of toys that are suitable for stimulating and vitalizing its formative activity. Toys with dead, mathematical forms alone have a deadening and desiccating effect on the child's formative forces. On the other hand, everything that kindles a sense of life works in the right way. Our materialistic age produces few good toys. For instance, a really healthy toy is the kind consisting of moveable wooden figures such as two smiths facing each other and hammering an anvil. You can still buy these in rural districts. Also excellent are picture books in which the figures can be set in motion by pulling threads from below, so that the child can himself transform the dead picture into a representation of living action. All this engenders a living mobility of the organs, and by such mobility the organs develop the forms that are right for them.

I can only touch on such things here, but in future anthroposophy will have to give detailed suggestions, and this is something it can do: it is not an empty and abstract doctrine but a body of living realities which can give guidelines that accord with life.

Let me just give a few more examples. A nervous or excitable child should be treated differently in terms of his environment and surroundings than one who is lethargic and listless. Everything can be considered, from the colour of the room and the objects that generally surround a child to the colour of the clothes in which he is dressed. If one does not look to spiritual knowledge for guidance one may often do the wrong thing, for in many cases a materialistic conception will lead people to hit on the exact reverse of what is needed. An excitable child should be surrounded by and dressed in red or reddish-yellow colours, whereas a lethargic child needs blue or bluish-green. The important thing here is the complementary colour which the child's eye creates itself. In the case of red the complementary colour is green, and in the case of blue, orange-yellow—as we can easily see by looking for a time at a red or blue surface and then quickly looking at a white surface. The child's physical organs create this contrary or complementary colour, and it is this which brings about the corresponding organ structures needed by the child. If the excitable child has a red colour around him, he will inwardly create the opposite, the green; and this activity of creating green has a calming effect, so that his organs assume a tendency to be more calm.

There is one thing that must be thoroughly and generally recognized for this stage of the child's life: the physical body creates its own inner measure for what is beneficial to it. It does this by the proper development of craving and desire. Generally speaking we can say that the healthy physical body desires what is good for it. In the growing human being, in regard to the physical body, we should pay the closest attention to what a healthy craving and desire seeks out. Pleasure and delight are the forces which best quicken and call forth the right physical forms of the organs.

Grave harm can however be done in this sphere by failing to bring the child into the right physical relationship with his environment. This can happen, particularly, in relation to the natural instinct for food. The child can be overfed with things that make him lose his healthy instinct for food entirely, whereas by giving him the right things to eat this instinct can be preserved. Then he will always want what is wholesome for him, down to a glass of water at the right moment, and turns away just as surely from what might do him harm. Spiritual science, when called on to develop an art of education, will be able to indicate all such things in detail, even specifying forms of diet and nutrition. It is a realistic approach to life that is drawn from life itself, and not a lifeless theory.

Thus the joy which the child has in and with his environment must be included in the forces that work formatively on the physical organs. He needs carers and educators with a cheerful manner, and above all honest, unfeigned love. A love which, as it were, streams with warmth through the child's physical environment may literally be said to incubate the forms of his physical organs.

The child who lives in such an atmosphere of love and warmth, and has around him really good examples to imitate, is living in his proper element. One should therefore rigorously avoid anything occurring in the child's presence that he should not imitate. One should never do anything in front of him which one would forbid the child himself to do. The strength of the child's tendency to imitate can be seen in the way he paints and scribbles written signs and letters long before he understands them. Indeed, it is good for him to paint the letters by imitation first, and only later to understand their meaning. Imitation belongs to this period when the physical body is developing, while meaning speaks to the etheric, which should not be worked on directly until after the change of teeth, once the outer etheric covering has fallen away. All learning to speak during this period should, especially, be through imitation. The child best learns to speak through hearing, and no rules or artificial instruction of any kind can have a good effect.

During early childhood it is important to realize the educational importance, for instance, of children's songs. They should make a harmonious rhythmic impression on the senses. Beauty of sound and tone rather than meaning is the important thing. The more living and lively the impressions made on eye and ear the better. Dancing movements in a musical rhythm have a powerful effect on building up the physical organs, and this too should not be undervalued.

With the change of teeth, when the etheric body lays aside its outer etheric integument, the period begins when education can work from without upon the etheric body. We must be quite clear what it is that can work from without upon the etheric body. The transformation and growth of the etheric body means the transformation or development of inclinations and habits, of conscience, character, memory and temperament. We can work on the etheric body through pictures and examples and by carefully guiding the child's imagination. Just as, before the age of seven, we have to give the child a physical model and example which he can imitate, so between the time of the change of teeth and puberty we must introduce into his environment things with the right inner meaning and value. It is from the inner meaning and value of things that the growing child will now take his lead. Whatever bears meaning, working through pictures and metaphors, is the right thing for these years. The etheric body will develop its forces if a well-regulated life of imagination can find its orientation in the meaning it draws from images and metaphors—

whether observed in real life or communicated to the mind. What works in the right way on the growing etheric body are not abstract thoughts but rather tangible realities—not of the external senses but of the imagination's inner eye. During these years, the right way to educate is by drawing on imaginative perception.

For this reason what matters most is that young people should have teachers to whom they look up, and who can awaken in them the right intellectual and moral powers. Whereas in the first period of childhood, imitation and example were, so to say, the magic words for education, so for the years of this second period the magic words are followership and authority. What the child directly sees with inner perception in his educators must become authority for him: not one compelled by force but one he accepts naturally and without question. By this means he will develop his conscience, habits and tendencies; by this means he will regulate his temperament. He will look upon the world through the eyes of this natural authority. Those beautiful words of the poet, 'Each of us must choose our hero, in whose footsteps we work our way upwards to the heights of Olympus', are particularly significant for this period of childhood. Veneration and reverence are forces through which the etheric body grows in the right way. If, during these years, it is impossible to look up to another person with unbounded reverence, one will have to suffer this loss for the rest of one's life. Where reverence is lacking, the living forces of the etheric body are stunted in their growth.

Imagine how an instance such as the following works upon a child's character. A boy of eight hears of someone who is truly worthy of honour and respect. All that he hears about him inspires a holy awe in the boy. Then the day comes when he will be able to see this person for the first time. With trembling hand he lifts the latch of the door behind which the person he reveres will be revealed. The beautiful feelings invoked by such an experience are among life's lasting treasures. Happy is he who can look up to his teachers and educators as to natural and unquestioned authorities—not only in specially elevated moments of life but continually.

Beside these living authorities who as it were embody intellectual and moral strength for the child, there should also be authorities whom he can apprehend only in mind and spirit. Outstanding historical figures, stories of the lives of great men and women, should inform his conscience and way of thinking. Abstract, moral maxims should not be used as yet: these only begin to have a helpful influence when the astral body emancipates itself from its mother-sheath at puberty.

The teacher should use history lessons in this way in particular. When telling stories of all kinds to young children before the change of teeth, our aim cannot be more than to awaken delight and vivacity, and happy enjoyment of the story. But after the change of teeth we can also bear something else in mind when choosing story material: that we are placing pictures of life before the boy or girl to kindle a spirit of emulation in the soul.

We should not overlook the fact that bad habits may be completely overcome by presenting appropriate pictures of qualities or character traits which the child finds repellent. Reprimands give little help at best in addressing habits and tendencies. If however we present a life-imbued picture of someone who has succumbed to a similar bad habit, and let the child see where such an inclination might actually lead, this will work upon the young imagination and go a long way towards eradicating the habit in him. We should always remember that it is not abstract ideas which influence the developing etheric body but the tangible experience of living pictures. The suggestion made here should certainly be carried out with great subtlety and tact so as not to reverse the desired effect. When telling stories everything depends on the art of telling. Oral narration cannot therefore simply be replaced by reading from a book.

In another connection too, presenting living pictures or, we might say, symbols and metaphors to the mind is important for the period of childhood between the change of teeth and puberty. It is essential that pupils absorb the secrets of nature as far as possible in living symbols rather than in dry, intellectual concepts. Parables and metaphors of the spiritual interconnections between things should be presented to the child's soul in such a way that underlying these he intuits and senses the laws of existence, instead of grasping things in a merely intellectual way. 'Everything transient is but a metaphor' should be the maxim guiding all our educational work at this stage.[11] It is hugely important for the child that his soul first experiences the secrets of nature in pictures and parables before he is led to understand them in the form of 'natural laws' and suchlike. An example may clarify this. Let us imagine that we want to speak to a child about the immortality of the soul, of its emergence from the body. The way to do this is to use a comparison, for example that of the butterfly emerging from the chrysalis. As the butterfly lifts from the chrysalis, so the human soul arises from the house of the body after death. Without first receiving it in such a picture, no one will properly grasp the fact in intellectual concepts. Such a metaphor or parable addresses not merely the intellect but the child's whole feeling and soul. A child who has experienced this will approach the subject with an altogether different mood of soul when he engages with it later in more intellectual concepts. It is actually a very grave matter if our first approach to the riddles of life is not imbued with a feeling response. Thus it is essential for the educator to draw on parables when presenting the laws of nature and the secrets of existence.

Here we have an excellent opportunity to see how spiritual science should affect practical life and make it fruitful. When a teacher comes before a class of children armed with concocted parables he has conceived intellectually, based on a materialistic outlook, this will generally make little impression on them. He has first had to devise these comparisons ingeniously and rationally, and when the intellect condescends in this way to create images they do not communicate convincingly. For when we speak in parable and picture, it is not only what is said and presented that affects the hearer, but rather a fine spiritual stream passing from one to the other—from the one who gives to the one who receives. If the person telling a story does not himself have the warm feeling of belief in his metaphor, it will make no impression on the other. To be really effective, it is essential to believe in one's parables as realities. And this can only be the case when we approach life from a spiritual perspective, and when the symbols and metaphors we use are themselves born from this outlook. Someone with a true spiritual outlook would not need to artificially force the metaphor given above, of the soul departing from the body, since it is reality for him. In the emergence of the butterfly from the chrysalis he sees, at a lower plane, the very same process that occurs at a higher level and higher stage of development when the soul emerges from the body. He believes wholly in this picture, and this belief as it were streams from speaker to hearer, carrying the power of conviction. Life then flows freely from teacher to pupil. But for this to happen it is necessary for the teacher to draw on the full fount of spiritual knowledge. His words and all that emanates from him must acquire feeling, warmth and colour from an authentic, spiritual-scientific outlook.

This opens up a glorious prospect across the whole field of education. By allowing itself to be enriched from the well of life that anthroposophy contains, education will itself be imbued with life and insight. The haphazard approach prevalent in this sphere will come to an end. All art and practice of education that does not continually receive fresh nourishment from roots such as these is dry and dead. Spiritual insights can find apposite metaphors and parables for all the secrets of the universe— drawn from the intrinsic nature of things, not first concocted by the human being but embedded in things themselves when they were created by the powers at work in the universe. This is why spiritual science must provide the living basis for the whole art of education.

A power of the soul which needs particular emphasis during this developmental period is memory. The development of memory is bound up with changes to the etheric body. Since the latter develops by emancipating itself between the change of teeth and puberty, so this is also the time when we need to make intentional external efforts to cultivate memory. If what is necessary here is neglected during this period, a person's memory will subsequently always have less value for him than it would have done otherwise. It is not possible to make good later what has been left undone.

Many mistakes can be made here by an intellectual and materialistic approach. Education based on such an outlook easily forms a prejudice against what it calls 'rote learning'. It will often tirelessly oppose the mere training of memory, adopting the most ingenious methods to ensure that boys and girls commit nothing to memory that they do not first understand intellectually. Yes, but how much is really gained by such intellectual understanding? A materialistic way of thought is so easily led to believe that one cannot penetrate further into things than grasping the intellectual concepts extracted from them. It has enormous resistance to seeing that other soul forces are at least as important as the intellect for comprehending things. It is not just a figure of speech to say that we can also understand with our feelings, emotions, our heart and soul, as well as with the intellect. Intellectual concepts are only one of the ways we have to understand the world, and only the materialistic thinker considers them to be the sole means of doing so. Of course there are many who do not regard themselves as materialists but who still think that an intellectual view of things is the only real form of insight. Such people may profess an idealistic or even spiritual outlook, but they relate to this in a materialistic way. Rational thinking is in fact the soul's means of grasping only material things.

We have already alluded to Jean Paul's excellent book on education, and I would here like to quote a passage from it, which relates to this theme of the deeper foundations of understanding. Jean Paul's book contains many a golden insight into education, and deserves far more attention than it receives. It is of greater value for the teacher than many of the educational works that are held in the highest regard today. The passage is as follows:

Do not worry that the child does not understand everything you say—even whole sentences. Your expression and the tone of your voice, aided by the child's intuitive eagerness to understand, will light up half the meaning, and with it, in the course of time, the other half. For children it is the same as for the Chinese and people of refinement: the tone in which you say something is half the language. Remember that the child learns to understand his own language before he ever comes to speak it, just as we do with Greek or any other foreign language. Trust to time and the context in which you say something to unravel the meaning. A child of five understands the words 'yet', 'even', 'of course', or 'just'—but now try to explain their meaning—not to the child, say, but to his father! The one word 'yet' embodies a miniature philosopher. If the child of three can understand the eight-year-old child, with his developed speech, why do you wish to narrow down your range of language to the infant's prattle?

Always speak to the child as if he were some years older: after all, geniuses speak to us in books centuries ahead of their time. Talk to the one-year-old as if he were two, to the two-year-old as if he were six, for differences in the child's development diminish in inverse ratio with his age. We are far too prone to credit teachers with everything that children learn. We should remember that the child we have to educate bears half his world already taught within him, the spiritual half, including for example a moral and metaphysical sense of things. For this very reason language, equipped as it is with material images alone, cannot give spiritual archetypes; all it can do is illumine them. Our joy and decisiveness when speaking with children flows as a matter of course from their own joy and decisiveness. We can learn from their speech as well as teach them through our own. Their word creations are bold yet remarkably accurate. For instance I have heard the following expressions used by three- or

four-year-olds: the 'barreler', the 'stringer' the
'bottler' (for the makers of barrels, strings and
bottles), the 'airmouse' (for the bat), 'I am the
see-through man' (when looking through a
telescope), 'I'm going to be even more cleverer',
'When I grow up I want to be a gingerbread-
eater-man', 'He joked me down from the chair',
'See how One it is' (on the clock) ... etc.

Our quotation refers, it is true, to a different
theme from the one with which we are concerned at present; but what Jean Paul says about
speech is also relevant here. In Jean Paul's
examples there is also a kind of understanding
which precedes intellectual comprehension. The
little child absorbs the structure of language into
the living organism of his soul, and to do so does
not need intellectual concepts of the laws of
linguistic structure. Similarly, the child between
the change of teeth and puberty must, to cultivate memory, learn much that he will not conceptually grasp until later. We best grasp in

concepts things which we have first learned just by memory at this stage of life, just as the rules of language are best learned in a language one can already speak. All the objections to 'unintelligent rote learning' are simply materialistic prejudice. For instance, the child only needs to learn the basic rules of multiplication in a few given examples—for which no calculator is necessary; the fingers are much better. Then he is ready to memorize the whole multiplication table. By proceeding in this way we take due account of the nature of the growing child, whereas we offend against it if, when memory development is the important thing, we call too strongly on reason and intellect.

The intellect is a soul force that is only born at puberty; before then we ought not to try to influence it externally. Up to puberty the child should use memory to acquire the treasures of human culture and thought. After this comes the time to penetrate with intellectual understanding what has already been impressed on the memory in earlier years. As well as remembering what we know, we must also gain insight into what we already know—that is, what we have acquired by memory in the same way the child first acquires language. This truth has wide application. First comes assimilation of historical events by memory, then exploration of them in intellectual concepts; first the committing to memory of aspects of geography, then intellectual grasp of their interconnections, etc. In a certain respect a conceptual grasp of things should be drawn from the stored treasures of the memory. The more the child knows through memory before he begins to grasp things conceptually, the better.

It should be clear by now that what has been said applies only to the period of childhood between the change of teeth and puberty, and not later. If at a later age one takes up a new subject, then of course the opposite might be true, and the most helpful way of learning may be through memory initially, though even here one cannot ignore each person's particular mentality. During the period with which we are here concerned, though, we should not desiccate the child's mind and spirit by cramming it with intellectual concepts.

Another effect of materialistic thinking can be found in lessons that depend too exclusively on sense perceptions. At this period of childhood, all perceptions need to be spiritualized. We should not be satisfied merely by presenting the child with a plant, seed and flower as this is visible to the senses. Everything should become a metaphor of the spiritual. In a grain of corn lies far more than meets the eye. A whole new plant lies invisible within it. The child should grasp in a living way, in his feeling and imagination, the fact that a seed, for instance, contains more than can be perceived with the senses. Through feeling he should intuit the secrets of existence. It is wrong to object that this obscures the senses' pure perception. On the contrary, by going no further than what the senses perceive, we stop short of the whole truth, for the full reality includes spirit as well as matter. There is no less need for faithful and careful observation when we bring all the soul faculties into play than when only the physical senses are used. If people in general could only see, as the spiritual researcher does, the desolation wrought on soul and body by a form of education that depends solely on sense perceptions, they would never insist on it as strongly as they do. What good, in the highest sense, is it to children to be shown all possible types of minerals, plants and animals, and all kinds of physical experiments, if this is done without connecting it with something else: with use of sensory metaphors and parables that awaken a sense of the secrets of the spirit?

A materialistic outlook, certainly, will make little of what I have said here, and the spiritual researcher understands this only too well. But he also knows that a materialistic outlook will never give rise to a really practical art of education. Practical as it seems to itself, materialistic thinking is impractical for entering into life in a living way. Materialistic thinking is a fantasy in relation to reality, despite the fact that a materialistic thinker will regard what spiritual science draws directly from life itself as fantastic. No doubt there are many obstacles still to be overcome before the life-imbued principles of spiritual science can penetrate the art of education. This is inevitable. As yet the truths of spiritual science seem strange to many. But if they are indeed true, they will eventually find their way into general culture.

Only by having a conscious and clear understanding of how specific educational measures work on the growing child can a teacher always find the right approach and timing to meet each instance in the right way. He needs to know how to treat the soul's various faculties—thinking, feeling and will—so that they develop in a way which works back in turn on the etheric body. In this period between the change of teeth and puberty, the etheric body can acquire an increasingly perfect state from measures brought to bear on it from without.

During the first seven years of childhood, the proper use of the educational principles we have discussed lays the foundation for developing a strong and healthy will, which is supported by the well-developed forms of the physical body. Then, from the change of teeth onwards, the etheric body as it develops endows the physical body with the forces that render its forms resilient and inwardly stable. At this period, whatever makes the strongest impression on the etheric body also works most powerfully to consolidate the physical body. The strongest affect on the etheric body is exerted by the feelings and ideas through which we intuit and experience our relationship with the depths of all existence—in other words through religious experience. A person's will cannot develop in a healthy way—and nor therefore can his whole character—if in this phase of childhood he cannot experience deeply penetrating religious impulses. How someone feels his place and part in the whole life of the universe comes to expression in the unified integrity of his will. If he does not feel connected to a divine spirit, his will and character inevitably remain uncertain, divided and unsound.

The world of feeling can develop in the right way through the metaphors and images we have referred to, and especially through imaginative pictures of great men and women which we draw from history and other sources, and present to children. Likewise a profound study of the secrets and beauties of nature is also important for proper development of feeling life. Last but not least is the cultivation of an aesthetic sense, and the wakening of artistic sensibility. The element of music must endow the etheric body with the sense of rhythm which then enables it to experience in all things the rhythm otherwise concealed. A child denied the blessing of having his sense of music cultivated during these years will remain the poorer for it throughout his life. If this sense is entirely lacking in him, whole aspects of life will inevitably remain a closed book for him. But the other arts should not be neglected either. The curriculum should make provision for awakening a sense of architectural forms, for modelling and sculpture, for a sense of line and drawing, and for colour harmonies and composition. However simple some of this might be in certain circumstances, there is simply no reason why something like this can't be done. The simplest means can achieve a great deal, as long as the teacher himself has the right artistic sensibility. A joy in life, a love of existence, strength and energy for work are some of the lasting effects of cultivating a sense of beauty and a feeling for art. How beautiful and refined human relationships can become under this influence! The moral sense which is also developing in a child during these years, through the way life is presented to him in pictures, through the natural authorities to whom he looks up, becomes assured and reliable if, through a developing sense of beauty, the child feels the good to be at the same time beautiful, and the bad to be ugly.

During this period of childhood, thinking as inner life lived in abstract concepts should remain in the background. It must develop of itself, as it were, uninfluenced from without, while the soul absorbs imaginative pictures of life and the secrets of nature. Thus between the age of seven and puberty, thinking and the faculty of conscious judgement is embedded, as it grows and ripens, within other soul experiences, so that after puberty a young person becomes able to form his own independent views of life and knowledge. The less directly the faculty of judgement is invoked in earlier years, and the more a good but indirect influence is brought to bear by developing other soul faculties, the better this will be for the whole of later life.

Spiritual science provides the right basis not

just for the spiritual and cultural aspects of teaching but also for physical education. Games and gymnastics can serve as an illustration here. Just as love and joy should permeate the child's surroundings during the earliest years of life, so physical exercises should give the etheric body an inner experience of its own growth and increasing strength. Gymnastic exercises, for instance, should engender in the child an inner feeling, with every movement or step, of growing strength within him. This feeling should take hold of the child as a healthy sense of happiness and ease. To devise gymnastic exercises that do this demands more than an intellectual grasp of human anatomy and physiology. It demands an intimate, intuitive knowledge of the connection between a sense of happiness and ease and the positions and movements of the human body. This kind of insight is not merely intellectual but is permeated with feeling. Whoever devises such exercises must be able to sense inwardly how one movement and position of the limbs produces a

64

happy, easy feeling of strength, while another gives rise to something like a loss of inner strength. To teach gymnastics and other physical exercises with this in mind, the teacher will need what spiritual science alone can give, and above all an outlook informed by spiritual science. He need not himself immediately be able to see into worlds of spirit. He just needs to have a sense of how to apply to life the insights derived from spiritual science. If spiritual-scientific insights were applied to practical spheres such as education, people would stop saying, quite idly, that spiritual science remains unproven. Just apply it and you will find that spiritual-scientific knowledge proves itself practically by making children strong and healthy. You will find that it does indeed hold good in practical life, and this will provide a proof more powerful than all logical and so-called scientific arguments can offer. Spiritual truths are best recognized by their fruits, and not by what is called 'proof', however supposedly scientific. Such proof, in fact, is little more than logical hair-splitting.

The astral body is not born until puberty. Only once it has freely unfolded can we also bring abstract ideas, the faculty for judgement and independent thought to bear from without. I have already said how up to this point these soul faculties should be developing free from external influences within the context of education appropriate for that earlier phase—in the same way that eyes and ears develop free from outer influences within the mother's organism. With puberty the time arrives when a person is ready to form his own judgements about the things he has already learned and committed to memory. We can do nothing more harmful to a human being than awaken his independent judgement too soon. A child cannot properly judge until he has inwardly gathered and stored material that forms the basis for judgement and comparison. If he forms his own conclusions before this, they will lack real foundation.

Educational errors of this kind lead to all narrow prejudice in life, to all barren professions of belief based only on a few scraps of knowledge, and a willingness to make shallow judgements about human ideas and experiences that have often proven their worth over long ages.

To be ready for mature thinking one must have acquired respect for what others have thought. Healthy thinking is always preceded by a healthy sense of truth built on faith in authorities we accept as a matter of course. If this principle were observed in education there would be fewer people who, believing they are ready to judge and discriminate too soon, spoil their own capacity to be open to all of life and allow it to work on them without prejudice. Every judgement that is not founded on soul treasures and experiences acquired in the right way creates a stumbling block for the one who forms it. Once we have pronounced a judgement on something, this influences our outlook ever after. We can no longer receive a new experience as we would have done if we hadn't already formed a judgement relating to it. The young person must have a living sense of the importance of first learning and then judging. The verdict of reason only comes after all the other soul faculties have spoken. Before then, reason only has a mediating role: its business is to grasp what occurs and is experienced in feeling, to receive it exactly as it is, rather than letting unripe judgement enter in and take possession. For this reason, up to puberty, the child should be spared all theories about things, instead simply experiencing life, and receiving these experiences into his soul. Certainly he can be told what different people have thought about this or that, but we must not encourage him to associate himself with a particular angle or view by exercising judgement too soon. He should absorb such opinions into his feelings. He should be able, without jumping to a conclusion or taking sides in an argument, to listen to everything and allow what each person said to resonate in him. Cultivating this kind of open mind in a child certainly requires great care and subtlety from teachers and educators, but such tact is exactly what a spiritual-scientific outlook can give.

I have only been able to pursue a few strands of this theme here, of education informed by spiritual science. My intention was simply to indicate how this outlook can approach its educational task in contemporary culture. Its power to fulfil this task will depend on an understanding of this way of thinking developing in ever wider circles of society. For this to happen, however, two things are needed. The first is that people abandon their prejudices against spiritual science. Whoever honestly approaches it with an open mind will soon find that it is not ridiculous nonsense as many people think. No reproach is intended here to those who believe this, for contemporary culture and all it is based on inevitably leads to the view, on first acquaintance, that adherents of anthroposophy are dreamers and fantasists. A superficial glance inevitably leads to such a judgement, making spiritual science appear to be wholly at odds with what modern education inculcates in people as the basis of supposedly healthy common sense. Only deeper reflection will show that contemporary views are themselves very contradictory, and will remain so as long as they are not rooted in a science of the spirit. By their very nature, in fact, they call out for the firm foundations of anthroposophy, and in the long run will make no headway without it.

The second thing that is needed concerns the healthy development of spiritual science itself. Only when it is generally recognized in anthroposophical circles that the insights of spiritual science must go beyond theory and become fruitful in the most far-reaching way for all aspects of everyday life, will life itself open to anthroposophy, coming towards it with sympathy and understanding. Otherwise people will continue to regard it as a type of religious sect for a few cranks and enthusiasts. If, however, it performs positive and useful spiritual and cultural work, the anthroposophical movement cannot in the long run fail to meet with understanding and recognition.

Notes

The text was first published as an essay in 1907.

1. Editor's note: Anthroposophy was the name Steiner gave to his wide-ranging Christ-centred philosophy and practice. Literally it means 'wisdom of the human being'. Steiner often uses this term interchangeably with 'spiritual science'.

2. Note by Steiner: This sentence does not imply that spiritual science is only concerned with the large issues. While it is true, as the passage above puts it, that spiritual science can offer the foundations for attempts to resolve *these* issues, it is also true that it can be the source for every single individual, whatever his position in life, of answers to the most common, daily questions, and of comfort, strength and confidence in his life and work. It can offer support in facing the great questions of life, but also in tackling the

most immediate needs of the moment, even in apparently insignificant concerns of daily life.

3. Rudolf Steiner: *Knowledge of the Higher Worlds*, Rudolf Steiner Press, 1969.

4. That is, plants.

5. Note by Steiner: This point needs to be stressed because there is a great lack of clarity about these things nowadays. Many people muddle the distinction between plants and sentient beings because they themselves are not clear about the real nature of feeling or sensation. If something reacts in some way in response to an external stimulus, this does not mean that it receives a sensation from the stimulus. It can only be said to feel a sensation if it *experiences the impression inwardly*; in other words, if there is a kind of inward reflection of the outer stimulus. The great advances of science in our time, for which the true spiritual researcher has the greatest admiration, have nonetheless introduced a lack of clarity as regards higher concepts. Some biologists do not know what sensation is and therefore ascribe it to an entity that has none. What they understand by sensation they can

equally well ascribe to non-sentient beings. Spiritual science understands sensation in quite different terms.

6. Note by Steiner: We should distinguish here between a person's own, inward experience of the astral body and perception of this latter by the trained clairvoyant. What is described here is the latter, as revealed to a seer's opened spiritual eyes.

7. Note by Steiner: The reader should not be offended by the expression 'I body'. It is certainly not used in any grossly material sense. But in spiritual science one has to use the words of ordinary language; and, since these are normally applied to material things, we first have to translate them into spiritual concepts.

8. Editor's note: This passage might seem offensive to modern readers fully conversant with principles of cultural respect and diversity, and generally admiring of ethnic cultures still partly 'unspoiled' by modern civilization. However, it is important to remember two things: firstly that Steiner was writing nearly a hundred years ago, in a quite different cultural and historical setting;

but secondly, and more importantly, that elsewhere he frequently makes clear that our higher ego development has also led to separation and alienation from nature and natural powers of insight. This ego development, he says, was inevitable and necessary, but also led to the dark age of materialism, from which we are only slowly emerging. When Steiner compares tribesmen with animals, we should also perhaps remember how greatly he admired animals, and how beautifully and sensitively he wrote about them (see, for example, his *Agriculture Course*). 'Higher development' therefore does not just mean 'better', but represents a further stage in a process which brings losses as well as gains.

9. Note by Steiner: To object that a child has memory and suchlike before the change of teeth, or that he has the faculties connected with the astral body before puberty, would be to misunderstand this passage. We must realize that the etheric body, and also the astral body, are present from the beginning, but that they are enclosed within their protective 'wraps'. It is, in fact, this protective covering which for example

76

enables the etheric body to evolve and display the qualities of memory very evidently before the change of teeth. But the physical eyes, too, are already present before birth, beneath the protective enclosure of the mother's womb. In the embryo the eyes are protected, and external physical sunlight cannot work on their development. In precisely the same sense, educational measures should not try to train or induce memory before the change of teeth. If, in contrast, we simply nourish memory without trying to develop it by external measures, we will see how it unfolds during this period of its own free accord.

The same thing is true of the qualities which the astral body sustains. Before the age of puberty we need to nourish them but always bear in mind that the astral body, as stated above, still lies within a protective enclosure. It is one thing to nurture *before* puberty the seeds of development already inherent in the astral body, but another thing, *after* puberty, to expose the newly independent astral body to the external influ-

ences which it can now receive and work upon,
unprotected by its enclosing sheath. The distinction is certainly a subtle one, but we cannot
fully understand the nature of education without
engaging with it.

10. Editor's note: Jean Paul (1763–1825), born
    Johann Paul Friedrich Richter, was a German
    writer best known for his humorous novels and
    stories. The book Steiner is referring to was
    published in 1807. An English edition under the
    title *Levana, or, The Doctrine of Education* was
    published 1863 by the US company Ticknor and
    Fields.

11. Editor's note: This motto first appears in
    Goethe's *Faust*. The original German is: 'Alles
    Vergängliche ist nur ein Gleichnis'.

Further Reading

Rudolf Steiner's fundamental books:

Knowledge of the Higher Worlds
also published as: *How to Know Higher Worlds*

Occult Science
also published as: *An Outline of Esoteric Science*

Theosophy

The Philosophy of Freedom
also published as: *Intuitive Thinking as a
Spiritual Path*

Some relevant volumes of Rudolf Steiner's lectures:

Study of Man
The Child's Changing Consciousness
A Modern Art of Education
The Essentials of Education
Rosicrucian Wisdom
Founding a Science of the Spirit

For all titles contact Rudolf Steiner Press (UK) or
SteinerBooks (USA):
www.rudolfsteinerpress.com www.steinerbooks.org

Other budget-priced volumes from Rudolf Steiner Press

Single lectures:
The Dead Are With Us
An Exercise for Karmic Insight
The Four Temperaments
How Can I Find the Christ?
How to Cure Nervousness
The Second Coming of Christ
The Work of the Angel in Our Astral Body

Meditations:
Breathing the Spirit, Meditations for Times of Day
and Seasons of the Year
Calendar of the Soul, The Year Participated
The Foundation Stone Meditation